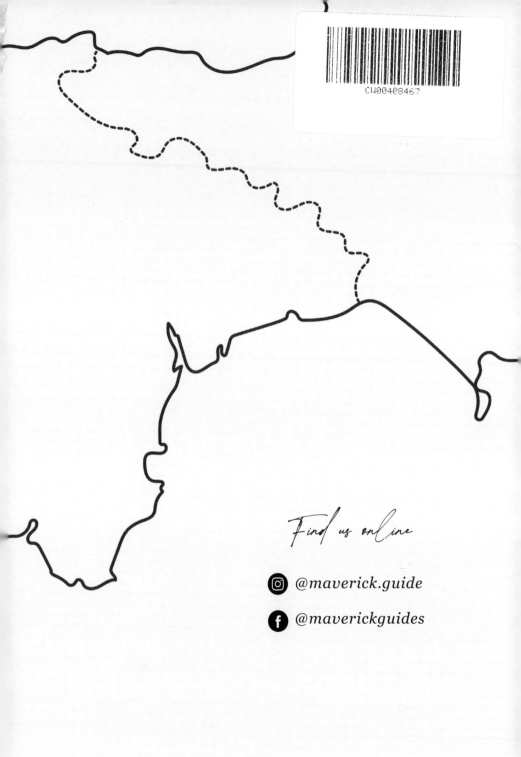

Find us online

:camera: @maverick.guide

:f: @maverickguides

EDITOR & GRAPHIC DESIGN

Gabriella Dyson

OUR TALENTED TEAM

Features Writer: Rachael Brown

Photography & Design: Ali Green

Sub Editor: Amy Kilburn

Recipe Development: The Cornish Chef

Illustration: Elin Mannon

With thanks to: Collette Dyson, Tom Litten

GET IN TOUCH

Editorial: editor@maverickguide.co.uk

Advertise with us: partnerships@maverickguide.co.uk

INSTAGRAM

@maverick.guide

MAVERICKGUIDE.CO.UK

Printed in Cornwall, UK. The Maverick Guide copyright © 2020

A Maverick

/mav(ə)rik/ | NOUN

A person who thinks and acts independently, often behaving differently from the expected or usual way.

"Dynnargh dhywgh"

...or in English: Welcome

The guidebook that you hold in your hands is the culmination of many personal trips to Cornwall, and many years of hard work and frustration. I have always longed for a guide to this region that truly encapsulates what makes it so special. Kernow is not just cheery seaside prints, pasties and Poldark. It's a county of extraordinary makers and proud, resilient people.

For every chain pub and mass-produced tea towel, there are hundreds of hard-working small businesses and hidden gems to uncover. It's a land of sensational scenery and a place where 'myths brush against reality'.

So, I invite you to join me in tossing aside run-of-the-mill guidebooks and embracing a new kind of attitude. Let's seek out like-minded people and indulge in everything that makes this county so brilliant...

Gabriella

Editor & Founder

Contents

INTERVIEWS

CULTURE & LIFESTYLE

Kudhva

tintagel

Initially an abandoned 45-acre quarry, Kudhva is a campsite with a unique ethos. Encouraging a more off-grid lifestyle, these architectural cabins promote a reconnection with nature, and they also offer sessions in surfing, wild swimming, foraging and outdoor yoga.

The 'Khudvas' (Cornish for hideaways) sleep two people and are raised up on four legs, putting you at eye-level with the treetops as they bristle around you. These hideaways are stylish yet purposefully minimalistic, gently nudging you to explore the surrounding scenery. And there is a lot to explore: woods, caves, heathland, waterfalls, the reservoir, the beach and, of course, the bar...

———

Sanding Road, Trebarwith Strand
Tintagel, PL34 0HH

kudhva.com

Hawksfield

Wadebridge

Few venues offer freshly roasted coffee, contemporary artwork, classic cars and sustainable fashion all in one place. But that's precisely why Hawksfield is one-of-a-kind. Located on the Atlantic Highway (A39) between Padstow and Wadebridge, Hawksfield has something for everyone...

Bespoke Traders specialize in sourcing rare, retro and exotic vehicles, including motorcycles, boats and other gentlemen's toys. There's also an eclectic mix of mens clothing and accessories, with brands such as Kytone and Peregrine along with genuine vintage biker apparel.

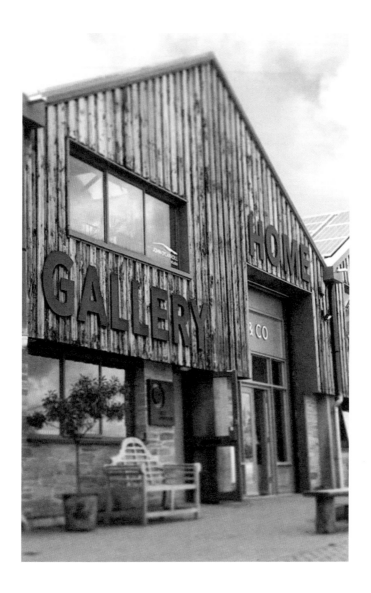

home & design

Design aficionados will be spoiled for choice at Hawksfield.

Seriously chic **Jo & Co Home** offers a curated selection of home accessories, women's fashion and gifts. Their new furniture showroom showcases bespoke sofas, armchairs and Farrow & Ball paint, all handpicked to help you create a living space you'll love.

A trip to **Cultivate** houseplant store is a *must* for anyone with green fingers. Emily Johnston's varied selection of houseplants include everything from tiny succulents to colourful orchids and marvellous *monstera deliciosa*.

food & drink

If you've worked up an appetite during your visit to Hawksfield, you should make **Strong Adolfos** your next port of call. These guys serve speciality coffee from Origin Coffee Roasters, as well freshly cooked breakfast and lunches, influenced by global cuisine.

There's also **ARC Speciality Food & Wine Store** onsite; a must-visit shop for any foodie looking to stock up on local ingredients, specilaist spirits, quality wines and gourmet gifts.

———————

Wadebridge, PL27 7LR

hawksfieldcornwall.com

Outlaw's Fish Kitchen

port isaac

Fish and shellfish from the surrounding waters dictate the menu at this intimate, eight table restaurant by internationally renowned seafood chef Nathan Outlaw.

Housed in a quirky 15th century fisherman's cottage, Fish Kitchen has more character than you can shake a stick at. Step inside and you're met with wonky walls, low ceilings, and only a handful of covers. But don't let the laid-back atmosphere fool you. The service here is top notch and Head Chef Tim Barnes cooks simple but refined dishes that have earned the restaurant a plethora of awards and accolades.

Outlaw's Fish Kitchen, photos by Collette Dyson

At Outlaw's Fish Kitchen, offerings arrive in the form of small plates designed for sharing. Four or five plates between two is generally the right amount (but you can order more as you go) and the dishes are kept simple but striking, with bold flavour combinations that bring them alive.

Port Isaac is home to some particularly narrow roads. So, we recommend parking at the top of the town and walking to Fish Kitchen. It's a great way to take in some of the stunning Port Isaac views...

───────────

1 Middle Street
Port Isaac, PL29 3RH

outlaws.co.uk

DISCOVER THE FINER SIDE OF CORNWALL WITH THE COWRIE CLUB

Our retreats are rooted in the astounding Cornish landscapes and the local communities that make them so welcoming. Our properties are specifically chosen for their unique locations, either on the dramatic cliff tops or the centre of idyllic communities. Your dream retreat awaits with The Cowrie Club.

thecowrieclub.com | *info@thecowrieclub.comw* | *01208 822186*

THE COWRIE CLUB

CORNWALL

Dining in
Padstow

Thanks to big names like Rick Stein and Paul Ainsworth, Padstow has become a firm fixture on Cornwall's culinary map. Famed for its fine dining credentials and known for serving some of the best seafood around, you'll be hard pressed to find a food lover who won't look forward to a trip to the popular coastal town. But with so many tempting options to choose from, how do you decide where to book?

RICK STEIN'S SEAFOOD RESTAURANT

Rick Stein's Seafood Restaurant has enjoyed an international foodie reputation since it first opened its doors in 1975. A dinner reservation here doesn't come cheap, but it's a must for seafood lovers keen to try the freshest catch of the day. We could quite happily have devoured everything on the à la carte menu and we recommend starting off your meal with some delicately sliced sashimi or six shucked oysters - served with cabernet sauvignon vinegar and a zingy shallot dressing.

Mains range from classic lobster thermidor to pan-Asian delights, and there's a particularly good turbot with hollandaise dish if you aren't watching your waistline. For something a little more theatrical, you ought to share the fruits de mer - a seriously impressive seafood platter piled high with half a lobster, crab, mussels, langoustines, scallops, oysters and razor clams.

The Seafood Restaurant, photo by David Griffen

PAUL AINSWORTH AT NUMBER 6

An evening at Paul Ainsworth's flagship restaurant is not easily forgotten. Housed within a beautiful Georgian townhouse, this Michelin starred venue lays right at the heart of Padstow and serves an innovative menu of modern British cuisine. Head Chef John Walton is a master of his art and the food coming out of this kitchen is next level. Lunch and dinner are both served as four course affairs, offering standout dishes like 'fillet of beef with bacon bearnaise' or 'Sladesdown Farm duck with umeboshi condiment and steamed dumpling'.

If you're looking for that perfect Instagram-worthy dish to round off your meal, you ought to order 'A Fairground Tale' for two. We won't ruin the surprise, but it's well worth forking out an extra £10 per person. With service and a wine list to match the level of the food, you'll want to book your reservation months in advance to secure a table.

BURGERS & FISH

If gourmet burgers are more your bag, 'Burgers & Fish' might be just the ticket. As the name suggests, this trendy restaurant in the centre of town specialises in one-of-a-kind burgers and unique fish dishes. They use a real charcoal grill to instil amazing flavour into their food and source only the freshest local ingredients for their plates.

GREENS OF PADSTOW

For a family-friendly option that's totally unique, head to Greens of Padstow. Starting out life as a pitch 'n' putt course, Greens is now half-restaurant, half mini-golf garden. Perched high above the harbour, with panoramic views of the town and Camel Estuary, you can work on your putting skills as well as tucking into lunch with a view. Dishes include everything from antipasti sharing boards to rib-eye steak or market fish of the day.

PRAWN ON THE LAWN

The last time we checked, these guys were off at nearby Trerethern Farm running a summer pop-up with local seafood and produce from Padstow Kitchen Garden. But depending on what time of year you catch them, their restaurant and fishmongers on 11 Duke Street is a fabulous little spot to snack on Porthilly mussels, fried oysters or whole lobster. We definitely recommend checking them out if you get the chance, but best check their website ahead of time to know where they'll be.

MUSSEL BOX

Overlooking Padstow quay, Mussel Box is a friendly little restaurant serving simple, delicious food that's fresh from the boat. We challenge you not to order a big bowl of mussels once you smell sizzling garlic and fresh parsley mingling with the salty sea air. Or better still, why not take a box of mussels away with you and eat them as you dangle your legs over the harbour wall.

Prawn on the Lawn

Ruby's Bar Padstow

BINTWO

Independent wine merchant BinTwo serves quality wines by the glass, as well as first-class Champagnes and some seriously good coffee. They also offer a small-but-perfectly-formed food menu, with dishes such as dressed Padstow crab and a classic Maine style lobster roll. Naturally, the focus is on the wines and these guys will be sure to match your meal with the perfect glass of vino. So, pull up a chair on their al fresco terrace and enjoy the sea air and harbour views.

RUBY'S BAR

If 1940s interiors and tasty cocktails float your boat, look no further than Ruby's Bar. Just a short stroll up from the harbour, Ruby's is another addition to Rick Stein's Padstow empire and offers a fantastic selection of gins, and cocktails such as Nitro Espresso Martini, Ceylon Negroni and Campari Fizz.

St Edmunds House

padstow

Boasting six of the most luxurious rooms Padstow has to offer, St Edmunds House takes coastal luxe to new levels. Set in its own private garden with views across the Camel Estuary to Rock and Daymer Bay, all six rooms offer four poster beds, oak flooring and American-style shutters.

Well-stocked mini-bars contain plenty of delicious local snacks, and spirits to quench your thirst - alongside Rick Stein's very own bubbly. There's also complimentary Origin Coffee, Birchall Tea and biscuits available to all guests.

Bathrooms feature Jill Stein's sumptuous Porthdune toiletries as well as pure white towels and freestanding baths for indulgent soaking. So, if you want to relax and unwind during your trip to the coastal town, a stay at this boutique venue should be high on your agenda.

St Edmunds Lane,
Padstow, PL28 8BZ

www.rickstein.com

LATITUDE
50

Rock I Daymer Bay I Polzeath I Port Isaac

Self-Catering Holidays On The Wilds Of The North Cornish Coast

However you plan to enjoy Cornwall, find the perfect base to come home to with Latitude50. Choose from cosy cottages sleeping four to beachfront homes sleeping twenty-eight and everything in-between.

latitude50.co.uk | holidays@latitude50.co.uk | @latitude50cornwallholidays

The Pig Hotel

harlyn bay

The Pig Group has a knack for transforming period
properties into coveted hotels, and it's first Cornish
venue is no exception. Once a 15th century mansion,
The Pig at Harlyn Bay is now a country house hotel,
boasting far-reaching sea views, oodles of charm and
plenty of original features.

Bedrooms are luxurious and characterful, with plush
velvets, freestanding baths and monsoon showers.
There are also four romantic Garden Wagons, full of
rustic reclaimed wood, cosy furnishings and log burners.

Dining

The Pig have a near obsessive commitment to homegrown produce and a love for all things local. So, you'll find menus that showcase ingredients fresh from the garden or from a 25-mile radius of the hotel.

Expect fresh-from-the-harbour seafood, award-winning English wines, hyperlocal cheeses and even Cornish saffron.

_____

Harlyn Bay,
Padstow, PL28 8SQ

www.thepighotel.com

DESTINATION
NEWQUAY

When you think luxurious vacations or tranquil retreats, Newquay rarely comes to mind. The colourful surfer's paradise has long-held a less than savoury reputation as the go-to destination for partygoers and budget holidaymakers... But thanks to its captivating coastlines and a myriad of trendy new venues, Newquay is starting to enjoy quite the transformation...

One of Newquay's biggest assets is its miles of sandy beaches. By far the most popular spot on the local map is **Fistral Beach** - one of the world's top surfing destinations. Hundreds of surf enthusiasts flock here each summer to get their big wave fix. The sunset is glorious at Fistral and deserves a mention of its own. Make sure you set aside time to catch the fiery oranges and vibrant purples that wash over the sky after the beach turns amber.

To truly make the most of the view, try stand up paddle boarding during golden hour.

Watergate Bay is another stunning beach to explore. Two miles of golden sand stretch out toward Newquay during low tide and impressive blue waves crash in from the Atlantic. To experience Watergate Bay in style, head to **The Watchful Mary** to feast on woodfired pizzas and sip on cocktails as the sun sets over the horizon.

Laid-back **Lusty Glaze** lies in a beautiful cove enclosed by dramatic cliff edges. The Restaurant & Bar is the perfect vantage point from which to gaze out to sea and listen to live music from Cornish musicians. **Holywell Bay** and **Porth Joke Beach** should also be on your north Cornwall itinerary and it's worth seeking out the curious poetic rock carving at **Piper's Hole** in Crantock.

Consistently good surf in the region means there is a choice of Surf Schools to choose from. **Fistral Beach Surf School, Quicksilver Surf School, Westcountry Surf School** and **Escape Surf School** all offer group and private lessons, or equipment hire on some of the most famous surfing beaches the country has to offer.

Looking for some new beach threads? Indie boutique **Roo's Beach** is a lively antidote to sometimes samey beach wear. They offer fresh, relaxed fashion and accessories suited to coastal living with lots of sustainable options. Delicate gold and silver designer jewellery, and colourful ethically-made beach bags are among our favourites.

On blustery days, nothing is more enticing than the display of meticulously decorated cakes and pretty bakes at Newquay's **The Basket.** All the packaging at this indie cafe is biodegradable and their salads and light bites are seriously delicious. There's also **The Jam Jar,** another one of Newquay's charming independent cake and coffee shops. Just a stone's throw from the beach, The Jam Jar's menu includes a wide range of organic teas, superfood smoothies, healthy breakfast bowls and freshly toasted bagels.

For something more substantial try **The Fish House**. Perched by Fistral beach, they serve seafood hauled in fresh from Newquay Harbour, arriving on your plate in the form of perfectly prepared mussels, grilled fish or fragrant risottos. Head Chef Paul Harwood has lived in Cornwall for over 25 years and learned his trade from none other than Rick Stein.

Come evening time, head straight to smart cocktail joint **Tom Thumb** to experience some cocktail alchemy. Expect combinations like citrus and spice, rose and hazelnut, and even rhubarb and custard on their creative drinks list. It's a classy spot that's worth visiting for their finely tuned, unusual flavours.

The Jam Jar, photos by Melanie Johnstone

The Scarlet Hotel

newquay

If it's relaxation you seek, look no further than The Scarlet Hotel. Overlooking the golden sands of Mawgan Porth Beach, this luxury eco-hotel is just for grown-ups.

That means you're free to unwind in their scenic meadow gardens or soak in a cliff top hot tub as the sun sets over the bay beyond. Each of The Scarlet's contemporary bedrooms boasts its own individual outside space; ranging from private garden terraces to balconies that open onto sweeping vistas.

relaxation

The hotel is also home to one of the
most coveted spas in all of Cornwall.
Rejuvenate in one of the tented
treatment rooms lit by lanterns or soak
in the ocean views from one of two
state-of-the-art swimming pools.
Find yourself slathered in rich mineral
mud or experience a traditional
bathing ritual in the hammam.

———————————

Mawgan Porthpotage, TR8 4DQ

www.scarlethotel.co.uk

Botelet

Liskeard

Hidden up-stream from Fowey, Botelet has been nurtured and styled by the Tamblyn family for over 150 years. It's the ultimate wellbeing retreat for weary city dwellers, offering nourishing massages and guided meditation sessions throughout the year.

Set among rolling wildflower meadows, you'll feel at one with nature in this authentic rural retreat. Sleep in one of three historic self-catering cottages or immerse yourself in the landscape in a Botelet yurt. Wake up to a homemade breakfast served at a long scrubbed-pine table and start the day the right way with simple, seasonal food and artisan coffee.

———————

Botelet, Herodsfoot
Liskeard, PL14 4RD

www.botelet.com

The Duchy of Cornwall Nursery

Lostwithiel

The Duchy of Cornwall Nursery is an enchanting garden nursery close to Lostwithiel. Arguably one of the most exceptional garden centres in the country - let alone in Cornwall - the nursery grows a creative selection of indoor and outdoor plants to fill your garden.

You can easily spend a whole afternoon browsing exotic houseplants in their glass house, wandering around the bumblebee garden, or contemplating the far-reaching views of Restormel Castle from their award-winning café.

The onsite shop is brimming with beautifully curated homewares, books and artisan gardening accessories. So, next time you're in the market for a stylish houseplant or an indulgent cream tea, you'll know exactly where to look...

_____

Cott Road
Lostwithiel, PL22 0HW

www.duchyofcornwallnursery.co.uk

Inside Alice in Scandiland, photo Rebecca Rees

Alice in Scandiland

Lostwithiel

This stylish brick-and-mortar store is brimming with objects that reflect owner Alice Collyer's love for minimalist and authentic Scandinavian design. Step inside and you'll be spoilt for choice by her curated selection of contemporary homewares, textiles and prints.

Vintage finds and mid-century furniture sit alongside artisan products, children's toys and Danish ceramics. Whether you're on the hunt for a bamboo magazine rack or a unique graphic print, you're bound to find something that takes your fancy.

---

28 Fore Street,
Lostwithiel, PL22 0BL

shop.aliceinscandiland.com

Photography by Ali Green throughout

A Weekend in Fowey

Strolling through the pretty streets of Fowey, it's little wonder why the town attracts a well-heeled sort of crowd.

Rows of smart tiered terraces overlook the wooded banks of the estuary, a myriad of galleries, independent shops and restaurants call its streets home, and Fowey's Readymoney Cove is the perfect little suntrap. It's easy to be won over by the white-washed lanes and unspoilt blue waters. But if you don't fancy relocating to the southern town just yet, you can always enjoy it for a weekend.

SHOPPING

Like every Cornish town, Fowey has its share of national chains. But it's also blessed with a number of independent shops and galleries. When seeking a little retail therapy, your first port of call ought to be **Brocante**.

With two shops on the town's main thoroughfare of Fore Street (and two more locations in St Ives and Mevagissey), Brocante is a lifestyle store designed for interior enthusiasts and those with a true appreciation of style. Filled with all manner of hand-picked home accessories, textiles and womenswear, you'll be spoilt for choice by the beautifully curated shelves.

Also on Fore Street, **Jo Downs Gallery** showcases stunning fused glass creations, from handmade gifts to statement interior pieces. **The Webb Street Company** is a quirky little store brimming with unique gifts and artwork, many of which have been sourced locally or have Cornwall and the sea at their core.

Elsewhere, **White Doll Arts** sell beautiful thrown pottery and whimsical ceramics; and **Pink Lemons Boutique** is your best bet for silk kimonos and delicate gemstone jewellery.

If it's food you seek, **Kittows of Fowey** should be your next stop. This charming, family-run butchers and delicatessen is brimming with all sorts of delicacies. There are designated meat and cheese counters along with homemade preserves, cakes and pies – many of which are made on their family farm.

Grab yourself a wicker basket and fill it with everything you could possibly need for a picnic; but save space for a quick trip to **Quay Bakery**. Here you'll get your hands on someof the best sourdough bread you've ever tasted (you have our word).

FOOD & DRINK

Nestled at the heart of Fowey's Fore Street, in a duck-egg blue, renovated townhouse is the newly moved and notoriously sleek **Appleton's Bar & Restaurant.** Bringing authentic Italian cooking to the harbourside town, settle down at their stylish bar and snack on sage and anchovy crispy bits or sip on elegant cocktails while you build up your appetite. For the main event, expect dishes such as home-grown mushroom and potato gnocchi, and zucchini flowers stuffed with local lobster.

The menu is filled with uncomplicated, downright delicious dishes that proudly highlight the best ingredients from Italy and the south west.

A little further down the road is fashionable **Fitzroy**, arguably Fowey's finest fine dining establishment. The menu here is all about sharing, so fill your table with with delicious small plates and feast on everything from velvet crab bisque to delicate choux buns.

Pintxo Tapas

Fitzroy's open kitchen gives you a front row seat to all the action, so you can sit back and watch the chefs at work as you sip on a glass of wine.

Over on 1 Lostwithiel Street, you'll find **Bufala.** This modestly-sized restaurant makes roman-style sourdough pizzas. Using lovingly sourced, authentic ingredients, you'll be hard-pressed to find thinner, crispier pizzas outside of Rome itself.

If you'd rather get away from the hustle and bustle of things, head to **Pintxo** on The Esplanade. This small but perfectly formed tapas and sherry bar is a hotspot for locals and is bringing a taste of España to the Cornish town. No reservation is necessary, just grab a seat and tuck into some seriously tasty tapas.

EXPLORE

Fowey has inspired its fair share of writers and artists. As the adopted home of Daphne du Maurier, traces of the famed thriller writer can be found all over the place. Nearby Menabilly Barton provided the inspiration for the haunting Manderley in her novel *Rebecca*, and numerous coastal and inland walks will allow you to walk in Du Maurier's footsteps as you explore hidden bays, creeks and woodlands.

Sir Arthur Quiller-Couch (the Cornish author known simply as 'Q') modelled his book *'The Astonishing Story of Troy Town'* on Fowey. For a taste of Q's Fowey, book a stay at **Artists House** on North Street, where the writer is rumoured to have lodged during his time spent writing about the town.

Readymoney Cove

When you've exhausted the picturesque scenery and had your fill of the local food scene, the best thing to do is take to the water.

Readymoney Cove is half a mile from the centre of Fowey, a small sandy beach sheltered by cliffs on either side. Sometimes, the beach can be submerged by spring tides, but during low tide you can take a dip in its crystal-clear waters or roll up your trousers and explore the rockpools.

On warmer days, you can paddleboard or kayak along the estuary. For novices, **Fowey River Expeditions** offer group river trips in canoes, so you can soak up the beautiful landscape from the water.

For adrenaline junkies, nearby Polkerris Beach is a great spot for windsurfing, with regular lessons available should you wish to learn a new skill.

Frequent ferries across the water will take you to the village of **Polruan**, a charming collection of cottages hugging the hillside. It's worth popping across for some excellent views of the local area from the top of Polruan Hill.

Alternatively, follow the creek a few miles north of Fowey and you'll arrive at the riverside hamlet of **Golant.** This modest little community is worth the detour for its riverside pub and excellent kayaking opportunities.

A small sandy beach
sheltered by cliffs on
either side

Retreat to Fowey

Retreat to Fowey's self-catering holiday homes are located just minutes away from Fowey's bustling harbour and picturesque estuary. These award-winning luxury apartments offer a stylish, laidback base from which you can enjoy your break in one of South Cornwall's most spectacular towns.

Sunlit **Apartment One** is the largest of the three apartments, comfortably sleeping six. The spectacular view of the estuary below fills the open-plan living room, with window-facing sofas positioned for you to drink it all in. Close by is the secluded Readymoney Cove and Polkerris beach is not far either. The latter is a great spot for paddle boarding, so why not hire a paddle board in town and make a whole day of it?

Apartment 2

Apartment Two benefits from stylish, cosy furnishings and a cool colour palette. Sleep in the master bedroom and you'll wake to a stunning floor-to-ceiling view of the estuary from the comfort of a kingsize bed. It's slightly higher on the hillside than Apartment One, so expect the views below to look as pretty as a postcard.

The apartment sleeps up to four people and, as with all the holiday homes, guests are welcomed with a hamper of Cornish goodies on arrival.

All lodgers also have unlimited access to the spa facilities at Fowey Hall Hotel just a short stroll away...

Old Station Master's House

Walk a few steps up from the river and you'll reach the beautifully furbished **Old Station Masters House;** a cosy and contemporary property for up to four guests.

At night, sink into a comfy bed in the stylish twin room or opt for the master bedroom that opens to an en-suite and private patio. In total, there are two outdoor tables for reconvening and relaxing after a busy day in the sea or pottering around the harbourside shops.

———————

www.retreattofowey.co.uk

01726 600029

Driftwood Hotel

Truro

For escapism and fine dining, Driftwood Hotel is just what the doctor ordered. The hotel is perched on the south west coast path, overlooking its own private beach and lush coastal gardens.

Decor throughout the hotel is what we would describe as 'New England coastal' and all but one of its fourteen bedrooms offer sea views and each boasts soft, luxurious bedding.

For total holiday bliss, check into Driftwood's rustic cliff-side cabin overlooking the bay. In true off-grid fashion, there's no Wi-Fi access or room service in the cabin, but it does benefit from access to the 'secret beach' and the hotel is only a short stroll away.

The restaurant at Driftwood is widely hailed as one of the best in Cornwall. Head Chef Olly Pierrepont and his team offer a seasonal, fine dining menu with some seriously stunning ocean views.

S W Coast Path, Portscatho
Truro, TR2 5EW

www.driftwoodhotel.co.uk

Sabzi Deli

Truro

Step into Sabzi Deli and you'll be greeted by rows of fragrant middle eastern dishes that are freshly prepared each day. Started by MasterChef quarterfinalist Kate Attlee, this colourful deli is known throughout Truro for its vibrant food and warm service.

Kate specialises in Persian delights that are bursting with flavour. So, be prepared to be spoilt for choice when you're presented with Sabzi's rainbow-coloured salads, hot lentil dahls and indulgent cakes...

Sabzi Deli also works hard to be as sustainable as possible. Making dishes from scratch creates less food waste and the packaging is always compostable. So you can have your fill of colourful takeaway, smug in the knowledge it's all ethically made too.

———————

Walsingham Place
Truro, TR1 2RP

www.facebook.com/sabzideli

Hotel Tresanton

St. Mawes

What was once a cluster of seaside cottages has been lovingly transformed into a characterful hotel by renowned hotelier and designer, Olga Polizzi. At its heart, St Mawes is a sea-faring community and this is beautifully reflected in Tresanton's style and location.

Each of the hotel's 30 boutique bedrooms and suites has been individually styled, many of which command splendid views across the water to the lush headlands of the Roseland Peninsula. Interior decoration is done exquisitely, with each room featuring a soft coastal colour palette and eclectic furnishings.

---

27 Lower Castle Road
St Mawes, TR2 5DR

tresanton.com

DESTINATION
FALMOUTH

With its colourful streets, golden beaches and thriving artistic community, Falmouth is a magnet for creative types and sun-seekers alike. Expect miles of coastal paths, plenty of independent eateries and some seriously laid-back vibes...

EAT

Falmouth's **Star & Garter** pub-with-rooms serves a menu of British classics for lunch and dinner, as well as hearty Sunday Lunches. Fish comes straight from the boat, while meat is fresh from the farm and butchered, cured and smoked onsite.

Chintz Bar is a fairground of cocktails and live music, usually brimming with cheerful characters. Walk through the cobbled courtyard and dive into a circus of quirky furniture and curiosities. It's not just a surreal trip into inebriation though: quality music, local ciders and artisan cheese boards make Chintz a must.

A pop of colour on Upton Slip, legendary crab and oyster bar **The Wheelhouse** sits on a narrow street that slopes towards the water. Fresh shellfish is caught and delivered daily and can be eaten by candlelight at this rustic spot. Quality of the service and the food is renowned far and wide, so booking is essential.

Resting on the harbour's edge, **Indidog** is an eatery with fantastic, blue harbour views. Inside the restaurant there's a tangible buzz and just outside is the calming flow of the water, changing colour throughout the day. Food here is excellent, especially their breakfast menu, with tempting vegan options and Bloody Marys.

Trot down a flight of steps to the underground French wine bar and brasserie **La Cave**. Run by a Cornish couple with a passion for French cuisine, La Cave has close, arched, candlelit ceilings that make for a cosy, intimate setting. Choose from their excellent menu or simply peruse through the generous list of fine wines and cheeses from France and Cornwall.

The Star & Garter Sunday Roast, Patrick Dowling

SHOP

We challenge you to pass by **Botanical Atelier** on Arwenack Street and not pop inside. This lovely little venue is run by local botanical artist, Sarah Humphries, and is stocked with a curated selection of interesting reads and plant-based homewares.

Smack bang opposite Sarah's shop you'll find the beautifully curated **Willow & Stone**. These guys sell all manner of lovely things, including traditional architectural ironmongery, stylish stationery and unusual gifts. If you're after a more sophisticated memento from your travels, this is where you'll find it.

Over on Market Street, you're bound to find something that catches your eye in **Uneeka.Life**. They're an ethical Cornish business and their shops are real treasure troves for homewares, furniture and gifts.

Fashion aficionados will also be spoilt for choice, with shops like **Parade** and **Finisterre** offering the finest threads, and vintage retailers like **Wild Pony** are on hand to give you your retro fix.

Walk a short way upriver to the harbour town of Penryn to find colourful homeware store **Just Delights.** Specialising in indie British and Danish brands, it's a grotto of gifts, furnishings and accessories. For lunch in Penryn stop at **Bango Kitchen**, a lively Asian fusion restaurant that rolls out delicious ramen, bao buns, katsu and sushi.

Botanical Atelier

PLAY

For the more adventurous, **The Cornish Diving Centre** can take qualified divers out for shore dives to search for the rays, jellyfish and cuttlefish that roam the Cornish waters. Friendly, professional staff also offer introductory courses for beginners to get you blowing bubbles.

WeSUP at Gylly Beach offer the chance to explore the ocean, coves and caves that surround it. Hire paddle boards, take taster or beginner lessons or experience a tour around the gorgeous Falmouth coastline. But don't worry, if you don't fancy getting into a wetsuit there are crystal-clear rock pools nearby, home to plenty of interesting sea creatures.

On the **south west coast path** there's a circular walk that begins in Falmouth and runs through the wooded pathways to Pendennis Point, offering striking coastal views. Another explores Mylor and Restronguet creeks, starting at Mylor Bridge, heading up toward Restronguet Barton, and following the curves of the water's edge back to where you started.

Hitch a ferry ride to the fishing harbour of St Mawes, a charming hillside town complete with a castle, whitewashed cottages and gastronomy spots. Some drinks on **The Idle Rocks'** waterside terrace is a great place to start. You could also pick up artisanal Cornish produce at **Mr. Scorse Deli** or discover the hidden cinema at **St Mawes Hotel.**

Every year plenty of festivals hit Falmouth that celebrate the area's maritime heritage. **Sea Shanty Festivals**, **Sailing Week** and, to mark the start of their fishing season, **Falmouth Oyster Festival** all burst onto the town. Unique to Falmouth, these occasions are lots of fun, but also offer an insight into Cornwall's proud culture.

The Star & Garter

falmouth

With enviable views of Falmouth harbour and a string of awards to its name, this pub-with-rooms certainly stands out from the crowd. World-class whiskey and rum dominate the drinks list, and the menu takes a "nose to tail" approach.

Upstairs, guests can book one of three gorgeous rooms: The Penthouse, The Crow's Nest or Starboard. Each suite boasts huge bay windows with sweeping views of the harbour.

Imagine spending an afternoon in front of the pub fire, getting engrossed in a good book and a delicious local cheeseboard, before heading back upstairs to your own private open-plan kitchen to cook up a feast of your own...

———————

52 High Street
Falmouth, TR11 2AF

www.starandgarterfalmouth.co.uk

Potager Garden

constantine

Stumbling onto Potager Garden Café feels like walking into a secret garden. It's brimming with greenery, bright flowers and ornamental shrubbery, and it's also a fabulous cake and coffee spot.

A team of dedicated volunteers help out with planting and landscaping at Potager, resulting in a beautifully cared for outdoor allotment and greenhouse garden. Inside, the greenhouse is lush and vibrant, with several chairs and tables spread out for afternoon teas and coffees. Meanwhile, the outside space is tranquil and welcomes both dogs and families.

Aside from delicious homemade cakes - lemon poppy seed catches our eye - expect 'Potager grown' dishes that are bursting with flavour, using ingredients that have just sprung up in the vegetable patch.

studios

Also nestled onsite are a cluster of artist studios, where if you time it right you may be able to catch an exhibition. Fitting with its community feel, the café holds regular craft workshops that are accompanied by fresh lunches and refreshments. The workshops aim to be fun while passing on skills and sustainable artistic practices like natural dyeing, pottery and printmaking.

Potager Garden occasionally host evening meals in the café. These are warm and cosy experiences with twinkling lights and delicious food. Although, if you want to experience them first-hand, be aware that they often sell out weeks in advance!

High Cross, Constantine
Falmouth, TR11 5RF

potagergarden.org

Inside Potager Garden, photos by Ali Green

Inside The Ferry Boat Inn, photo Mae Pate

The Ferry Boat Inn

helford passage

Sitting in an unspoilt cove, with direct access to the water,
The Ferry Boat Inn overlooks one of Cornwall's most magical
places: the timeless Helford Passage. Arrive here by water
to truly soak up the scenery and enjoy a drink on the terrace
for some of the best views around.

Inside, The Ferry Boat Inn has strong a nod to its nautical
roots; with vintage pictures of old sailboats hanging from
the walls, traditional panelling and a hand-crafted oak bar.
Where food is concerned, you can expect delicious pub
fayre, with signature dishes such as mackerel tacos and
tried-and-tested classics such as fish & chips and
Sunday roast.

Helford Passage
Falmouth, TR11 5LB

www.ferryboatcornwall.co.uk

New Yard Restaurant

Helston

New Yard Restaurant is housed in the former stable yard of Trelowarren Estate. In keeping with its unique location and historic credentials, casual laid-back dining is the name of the game. With a menu guided by the seasons, you can expect innovative dishes made with locally sourced produce and ingredients from their own walled garden.

Food is refined but unfussy, with dishes such as nettle and spinach tortellini and monkfish roasted in butter, served alongside rustic sourdough loaves and woodfired pizzas.

Inside NYR photo by Adam Sargent

Cured monkfish photographed by Caroline Robinson

the food

In the balmy summer months,
drinks can be enjoyed al fresco
in the courtyard, and when
there's a chill in the air diners are
invited to sit by the roaring fire.

The Pantry, a former stable which
belonged to the dining room's
coach house, is situated next
door to the restaurant. Head here
for homemade bagels, pastries,
breads and cakes, along with
coffees and their very own cider.

———————

Trelowarren, Mawgan
Helston, TR12 6AF

newyardrestaurant.co.uk

St Ives' Harbour, photo Collette Dyson

Exploring St Ives

St Ives requires no introduction. Slanted slate roofs and twisting cobbled lanes, little fishing boats bobbing on the water...

It truly is a picture-perfect Cornish town. But thanks to its tea-towel-worthy credentials, it's something of a tourist hotspot and it pays to plan your visit in advance...

SHOPPING

St Ives' winding streets are filled with indie shops to explore; offering everything from fudge to artisan pottery, fine jewellery and local art.

The Painted Bird is a good place to start. This charming little shop is filled with all manner of homewares and gifts, including handwoven cushion covers, recycled leather purses and delicate dried flower bouquets.

On St. Andrew's Street, you'll find **Magpie & London** nestled among the galleries and backstreet bistros. Shop to a soundtrack of 90s R&B and browse their beautifully curated selection of jewellery and accessories. We're particularly fond of their signature 18ct gold plated seahorse pendants: each one is individually made and completed by your choice of gemstone.

Of course, not all that glitters is gold. Elsewhere on St Andrew's Street you'll find **Emjems**: a treasure trove of crystals and jewels. Inside, almost every surface glitters with strings of semi-precious stones, sparkling geodes and intricate silver jewellery. The shop is filled with the aroma of incense and essential oils, including their own heady blend of 'Pirate Oil'.

Only a short stroll away there's **JOHNS Wine & Spirits.** One of Cornwall's longest-running family businesses, it stocks a range of rare and unusual spirits, including a number of unique Cornish drinks. So, if you're shopping for a quaffable souvenir look no further.

We guarantee that **St Ives Bakery** will stop you in your tracks. This unique, glass-fronted bakery is quite the sight, with a window display stacked high with colourful meringues, flaky pastries and traditional pasties. You'll be drawn inside by the aroma of freshly baked bread and we doubt you'll be leaving empty handed...

EATING OUT

The Rum & Crab Shack is a popular spot with locals, thanks to delicious dishes such as crab tacos, rum-covered ribs, and cajun fish burgers. As the name suggests they also offer an extensive cocktail menu and a huge variety of rums to choose from, including their own Cornish rum: *Dead Man's Fingers.*

Alternatively, you could seek out fresh sushi and vibrant poke bowls at **The Searoom**: a cocktail bar and tapas restaurant sitting right on the harbourfront. These guys serve up some excellent Asian-inspired dishes, as well as some particularly tasty souped-up chips (think crabmeat and cheese sauce). Owned and run by the minds behind St. Ives Gin, it should come as no surprise that alongside wine and craft beers, The Searoom specialise in G&Ts. We recommend the Super Berry Gin, served with sea buckthorn, blackberry and honey tonic.

The Searoom

Porthminster Beach Caf

Elsewhere, **Porthminster Beach Café** serves up its own playful take on Cornish cuisine. They've stripped out much of what they deem unnecessary, so dairy and gluten take a backseat in favour of fresh and exciting textures and flavours. Head here for panoramic views of Porthminster Beach and relax on the sun-drenched terrace during the warmer months.

Located just below The Tate St Ives, **Porthmeor Beach Café** has a buzzing atmosphere. Their famous 'build your own breakfast' usually hits the spot, they also have an extensive vegetarian menu and some lovely seafood tapas.

A trip to St Ives wouldn't be complete without sampling the local ice cream. So, make sure a trip to **Moomaid of Zennor** is on the cards. This family-run business creates luxury ice-creams from their dairy farm on the cliffs between Zennor Hill and The Atlantic Ocean. Their St Ives harbourside parlour serves a myriad of flavours, including our favourite flavour 'Ship Wreck': a decadent sea salt ice cream made with dulce de leche caramel and honeycomb.

THE ART SCENE

St Ives is legendary for having exceptionally good light. So much so, the town has become a mecca for Cornwall's artistic community. **The Tate St Ives** and **The Barbara Hepworth Museum** are both compulsory destinations for art lovers; but there's also an assortment of small independent galleries that call the town home.

One of our favourite galleries has to be **Belgrave St Ives.** It's the only private art gallery in Cornwall showing regular exhibitions of work by major artists associated with the St Ives Modern Period. The gallery is unpretentious and informative, meaning its friendly staff are always on hand to discuss the art on display.

Of course, if you want to work with the extraordinary light first-hand, you can dive into a practical workshop at one of St Ives' many art schools and classes. Established in 2015 by artists Zoe Eaton and Peter Giles, **Barnoon** is a small dedicated art space in the heart of the town. Surrounded by beautiful scenery, overlooking Porthmeor Beach, the workshop is located within minutes of the South West Coast Path, as well as the Tate. You can book yourself onto a number of creative classes, from beginners calligraphy to contemporary decoupage.

St Ives School of Painting provides expert tuition for all levels, from complete novices through to budding Picassos. The studios themselves have recently benefitted from a modern facelift, with floor length windows overlooking the ocean and contemporary skylights basking the studios in natural light. The school offers weekend courses, so you can combine a trip away with a chance to develop new skills. Learn the basics of oil painting, improve your landscapes, or opt for one of the frequent 'alumni sessions' to learn from seasoned experts.

For ceramic lovers, a visit to **The Leach Pottery** should be high on your to- do list. Established by friends and colleagues Bernard Leach and Shoji Hamada in 1920, The Leach Pottery was built on a foundation of experimentation. Over a century later, visitors can learn how to throw their own pottery creations with a range of hands-on courses.

St Ives School of Painting

Porthminster Beach

THE BEACHES

Thanks to its irregular-shaped coastline, there are plenty of beaches to explore in St Ives. The town's Blue Flag beaches are some of the best destinations for surfing and windsurfing in the country, but you'll also find a number of sheltered inlets that are ideal for sunbathing and quiet strolls.

The most popular local spot is **Porthmeor Beach**: a favourite of surfers and family's alike. Westerly rockpools will no doubt keep the kids entertained, while adults can take advantage of the clean sands and amazing surf.

Porthgwidden Beach is a small sandy cove on the opposite side of the headland to Porthmeor. It's an ideal spot for sunbathing and a dip in the ocean, as it's sheltered from the wind and the waves that batter Porthmeor.

Located right by the train station, you'll find **Porthminster Beach:** a long sandy beach with a backdrop of beautifully maintained lawns. A regular recipient of the Blue Flag award, Porthminster is ideal for young families, thanks to its first-class facilities and its calm, lifeguard patrolled waters.

Squint and you'd be forgiven for mistaking the glorious **Carbis Bay Beach** with the white shores of the Mediterranean. Just one mile east of St Ives, this sensational beach boasts beautiful turquoise waters.

Harbour view House

st ives

As its names suggests, each of Harbour View House's rooms boast stunning views of St Ives' harbour and the vibrant seaside town. After functioning as a B&B for 40 years, the boutique hotel has been lovingly updated with second-hand, repurposed furniture and stylish accessories sourced from the owner's travels.

Downstairs you'll find **Hatch Café**: a seriously Instagram-worthy venue with arthouse prints on the walls, a retro-looking coffee machine and lush houseplants. With a chef who honed their skills in Sydney, the menu here is reminiscent of a cool Australian eatery; featuring all-day breakfast burritos and colourful fruit bowls.

———————

Fernlea Terrace
St Ives, TR26 2BH

www.harbourviewonline.co.uk

Primrose House

st ives

This charming boutique hotel is just a stone's throw from
St Ives' picturesque harbour and Porthminster Beach.
Once an impressive Edwardian townhouse, the building
has been part of the St Ives community since 1908
but has benefited from a thoroughly modern facelift
in recent years. Most of the hotel's eleven bedrooms
and suites feature king-sized beds, along with a muted
coastal colour palette, exposed-stone walls, stylish
textiles and plenty of little luxuries.

———————

Primrose House,
St Ives, TR26 2ED

www.primroseonline.co.uk

boutique
RETREATS

From raising the flag on your own private island and sailing a boat to your cottage, to watching the stars over the sea from your hot tub, Boutique Retreats specialise in unique, stylish properties that celebrate their surrounds whilst embracing luxurious living.

Whether you're after something large and luxurious or beautifully bijou, a long weekend or a two week summer holiday, our carefully selected properties will take your breath away.

We know how good getaways should be.

The Jubilee Pool

Penzance

The Jubilee Pool is the largest sea water pool in the UK:
a unique lido situated right on Penzance seafront.
Designed in the early 1930s by Captain F Latham, the pool
was made to withstand the full ferocity of the Cornish sea,
while its sweeping curves and art deco architecture provide
a stylish and laid-back venue for swimmers.

The pool is closed during the winter months (open from
May to September) but during summer, the Poolside Café is
a great spot to grab a coffee – or a craft beer – and take in
the panoramic views of Mount's Bay.

———————————

Jubilee Pool, Battery Road
Penzance, TR18 4FF

www.jubileepool.co.uk

Jubilee Pool by Leon Foggitt

Mousehole Harbour by Ali Green

HEAD WEST

It's a well-known fact that the further west you travel, the wilder Cornwall becomes. The Atlantic Ocean batters the shoreline, and ancient moorland and gorse-topped cliffs are punctuated by tiny fishing villages and abandoned mine stacks. So, if it's an authentic Cornish experience you seek, consider heading west...

PENZANCE

Penzance draws in considerably fewer crowds than its stylish counterpart, St Ives. But in recent years this westerly town has really come into its own. Today, a number of small galleries, boutique hotels and artisanal businesses call its historic lanes home.

In recent years Penzance has gained significant recognition within the Cornish art scene. **The Exchange** on Princes Street is little sister to nearby Newlyn Art Gallery; an internationally renowned institution that has been bringing world-class art to south west England for over 120 years. In its former life, the building acted as the town's telephone exchange, so The Exchange retains its original industrial feel. The gallery has exhibited major works from international and national artists, along with community-based exhibitions celebrating local talent.

At the top of historic Chapel Street, you'll find Cornwall Contemporary. Opened in 2006 by Sarah Brittain-Mansbridge, this bright and spacious gallery is set out over three floors and show-cases the work of established and highly respected artists, alongside work by up-and-coming art school graduates.

Of course, art lovers and nature lovers alike should discover **Tremenheere Sculpture Gardens.** In a sheltered valley, not far from Penzance, renowned artists James Turrell, David Nash and Richard Long have combined subtropical planting with unique modern art installations. As well as the sculpture gardens themselves, Tremenheere offers an excellent café, gift shop and plant nursery (specialising in rare and unusual succulent varieties).

The Artist Residence

The western tip of Cornwall is a food lovers paradise, with freshly caught seafood in abundance and plenty of award-winning restaurants.

The most coveted venue in town is **The Shore**, overseen by Bruce Rennie. This celebrated restaurant offers a small and ethically sensitive menu, with an emphasis on seafood and fresh, local produce. Expect fish straight from the day boat and vegetables from nearby growers.

A small but well-formed wine list accompanies the menu, along with a selection of unique gins and locally crafted beers.

Elsewhere, **The Clubhouse at The Artist Residence** serves smoked and wood-fired local cuisine from their cosy, timber-clad venue. **The Cornish Hen** deli is the perfect place to stock up on local produce, and **Totti** offer simple but delectable Neapolitan pizzas.

NEWLYN

The fishing village of Newlyn is only a brisk 20-minute walk along the seafront from Penzance. Its historic harbour is world famous for its fishing fleet and has been in use for hundreds of years (The Mayflower even stopped here in 1620 on its voyage to the New World).

Thanks to its top-notch fishing credentials, you'll find some of the best seafood in Cornwall here. Chef Ben Tunnicliffe eschewed the fine-dining label and opened **The Tolcarne Inn** back in 2012. Now headed by Matt Smith, you can expect a daily updated blackboard menu showcasing the catch of the day and seasonal ingredients from local community farms and market gardens. Listen to the tinkling sounds of fishing boats outside as you sit by the fireside and soak up the traditional atmosphere with a pint of real ale among the locals.

Movie buffs will no doubt love **The Newlyn Filmhouse.** Set in the converted JH Turner & Co fish merchants building, this indie cinema screens everything from the latest mainstream films to art-house pictures.

The Tolcarne Inn, Newlyn

Everywhere you look there are traces of the building's past, brought up-to-date with contemporary furnishings and objet d'art. The onsite restaurant and bar are both worth a visit in their own right, with eccentric décor, an eclectic menu and a good selection of drinks.

Coastal footpaths wind their way out of the village, offering plenty of spots for sea swimming or paddling. Newlyn's little-known beach, Sandy Cove, is also a great spot for shell-hunting or combing the pebbles for beautifully polished sea glass.

MOUSEHOLE

Few places are as quintessentially 'Cornish' as the tiny fishing village of Mousehole. Just a 15-minute drive from Penzance (or an hour or so walking, if you want to brave the coastal air), Mousehole is blessed with outstanding views, great surf and some seriously gorgeous holiday rentals.

The only watering hole in Mousehole is **The Ship Inn**: a busy little pub that's part of the St Austell Brewery family. The food is fairly standard pub grub, but they pull plenty of pints and serve some great local ales and ciders. Want to book the best restaurant in town? That would be **2 Fore Street.**

It's got a laid-back bistro vibe and is situated right on Mousehole harbour. Menus change regularly, so there's always something to take your fancy, whether that's a hand-picked crab salad or lemon sole fillets with salty samphire.

Mousehole is a community that holds steadfast to its traditions. Every December, its picturesque harbour is illuminated by hundreds of twinkling Christmas lights. Visitors travel from far and wide to watch the town light up and locals have fondly dubbed the proceedings 'Mouse Vegas'.

The Minack Theatre, Mike Newman

ST MICHAEL'S MOUNT

St Michael's Mount is a magical little tidal island crowned by a medieval castle. After a steep climb to the top, you'll be rewarded with outstanding views and beautiful island gardens. The Mount's historic stone walls harbour a multitude of plants, from tiny succulents to giant agaves. Inside the castle, you can wander century-old corridors and unravel the history of the St Aubyn family, who have lived on St Michael's Mount since the 17th century. Since the island is owned by The National Trust, make sure you remember to bring your pass with you; else the entry fee is £16pp

THE MINACK THEATRE

Follow the coast round to Porthcurno and you'll find one of the most extraordinary places in all of Cornwall: The Minack Theatre. Lovingly carved into a hunk of cliff, The Minack Theatre offers magical performances against the backdrop of the Atlantic Ocean. Its dramatic setting and stunning views of Porthcurno Bay are well worth experiencing, however excitement at The Minack comes from its open-air performances. There's something quite special about watching a cast of actors perform their art as the sun sets behind them and the stage lights up in technicolour.

LANDS' END

When you hit Lands' End you've gone as far west as possible without getting your feet wet. Congratulations. Why not get your photo taken at the famous Lands' End sign or pay a visit to one of the area's many tourist spots? Here you'll find interactive amusements 'Arthur's Quest' and 'The End to End Story', as well as Greeb Farm and the West Country Shopping Village. Personally, we prefer to savour the rugged coastline and striking sea views with a brisk coastal walk - each to their own.

The Artist Residence

Penzance

The Artist Residence is a luxurious little boutique hotel full of creative and colourful artworks - some hanging on the walls, others for sinking into. Think brass freestanding baths, deep leather armchairs and patterned fluffy shag rugs. In ten minutes you can be at the Penzance seafront or taking a brisk swim in the art deco Jubilee Pool.

Alternatively, opt to stay onsite to soak up the buzz from the outdoor wooden terrace, dotted with plants and fairy lights. The atmosphere is relaxed, punctuated with the sound of ping pong and drinks clinking from the alfresco bar. Inside in the lounge, sofas are gently warmed by a glowing log burner.

The Clubhouse

The Artist Residence's friendly
downstairs areas: the lounge,
garden, bar and smokehouse,
make up 'The Clubhouse', the
sociable heart of the hotel.
Sip cocktails here and graze
on some seriously tasty dishes.
The menu is full of inventive
twists on classics, like squid
with lemon saffron aioli or
apricot soy chilli chicken wings.

———————

20 Chapel Street,
Penzance, TR18 4AW

artistresidence.co.uk

Chapel House

Penzance

Chapel House Penzance is a boutique hotel that boasts six light and spacious double bedrooms. Each room offers guests large, handmade oak beds and state of the art en suite bathrooms (with sink-down-deep baths or waterfall showers). All rooms have sea views and three of the six have large sea-facing windows giving impressive views over Penzance harbour and Mount's Bay as far as Lizard Point.

From 6.30pm to 8.30pm every Friday and Saturday, enjoy early evening drinks (free for house guests) before sampling their Kitchen Supper, served from 7.30pm to 10pm.

———————

Chapel Street,
Penzance, TR18 4AQ

chapelhousepz.co.uk

Harbour Moon

mousehole

Harbour Moon is a particularly special one-bedroom holiday cottage in the picturesque village of Mousehole. This cosy lodge is located right on the harbour, so expect to watch little boats bobbing on the horizon while sinking into the sofa.

Light will form an important part of your stay, particularly since part of the bedroom floor is made of glass. The open plan living area is styled with Mousehole's maritime heritage in mind, with its stone walls exposed and soft colour palette. Muster up the strength to leave the wood burner and you'll find shops, art galleries and pub lunches, all within a couple minutes walking distance.

———————————

sandandstoneescapes.com

the CERAMICIST

In a modest little studio at the bottom of her garden, you'll find Julia Crimmen busy at her throwing wheel or painting details onto her delicate porcelain creations.

Julia is a ceramic artist whose whimsical work draws inspiration from the Cornish Coast and the hedgerows that grow by her home in the village of Porkellis. Her stoneware mugs, porcelain animals and hand thrown planters perfectly capture the spirit of Cornish design...

STARTING OUT IN CERAMICS

In 2006 I signed up for a *Diploma in Art & Design* at Falmouth University, as a mature student. At first, I thought I would be a print maker, as I loved the process. But in the final term, I discovered a bag of clay in the Marine School and I was hooked. I followed this course with two years of *General Ceramics* at Truro College and some wonderful intensive courses with local experts such as Jack Doherty, Linda Bloomfield and Richard Phethean.

MY GARDEN STUDIO

The stroll to my garden studio is the perfect commute and I can often be found working in the early morning in my pyjamas. It's not really a 9-5 type of career but having the studio at home means I can pop out and load the kiln in between jobs around the house. A couple of years ago, we built another little 'show shed' here the garden, which I use to display finished pieces (open to the public by appointment). But, no matter how much space I have, I still end up with work drying in the kitchen!

MY CREATIVE PROCESS

I use a sketchbook to design new shapes, but I'm also influenced by the ceramics I use every day. I've got certain cups and mugs I like to use for certain drinks or certain times of day. Am I the only one who does this? Maybe I'm a bit odd, but I like to make a variety of different shaped vessels: shapes that feel comfortable in your hand, handles that can hold more than one finger, and tactile glazes and textures.

THE INFLUENCE OF CORNWALL

This county inspires me a lot. I'm always much more creative after a good walk along the coast and my porcelain pieces have textures and colours inspired by these strolls. The local stoneware clay I use gives me the freedom to make larger pieces and with that comes a looser style of decoration. The rich indigo blue and white designs I create really reflect coastal living and I hope my work shows the joy I feel creating it.

MY FAVOURITE PLACE

My family ran the farm at Church Cove in Gunwalloe for over 50 years, so growing up there means it will always be a very special place for me. My husband and I were married in the church on the beach and we have lots of lovely memories of family holidays there. Rain or shine, it's a very beautiful place.

CORNWALL IS FULL OF TALENT

I love Sarah Eddy's beautiful paintings, with their rich colours, her coastal images are just stunning. Lin Lovekin makes the most gorgeous wicker baskets, lampshades and homewares. Sarah Drew's jewellery is just lovely, and Amy Cooper's amazing porcelain lighting is a real reflection of our gorgeous county

.

You can find Julia's work in a number of galleries, such as Four Crows in Porthleven, The Penwith Gallery in St Ives and Circa 21 in Penzance. You can also browse her work online: juliacrimmenceramics.co.uk

Sleeping in Ferns by Elin Mannon

ILLUSTRATOR
the

Ancient ruins, fair maidens and kingdoms lost beneath the sea are all themes that have featured in Elin Mannon's colourful artwork.

An illustrator and recent graduate of Falmouth University, Elin's work is inspired by the social history and natural landscape of Celtic regions, such as Wales and her adopted home of Cornwall. Her work has graced the pages of story books and illustrated a myriad of folkloric tales...

I WAS ALWAYS A CREATIVE CHILD, WHO LOVED TO DRAW & PAINT THE WORLD AROUND ME...

I remember getting very excited about my drawings as a child; eager to show my parents what I had created from my imagination Like many creative people, I studied art all the way through school, but I quickly noticed that it was viewed as a 'soft subject' or a 'throwaway class'. This meant that I was never really given the opportunity to explore what options were available to me if I wanted to pursue an artistic career.

INITIALLY I WAS GOING TO STUDY HISTORY AT EXETER UNIVERSITY.

But toward the end of sixth form I was encouraged by my family to defer my degree and take a Foundation Diploma in Art. It was where my passion really lay and it was important not to close those creative doors. It still scares me to think what my life could have turned out like if I'd gone down that more 'traditional' route.

I LOVE STORYTELLING.

Not just committing words to a page, but literally taking an idea or a concept and telling stories through my art. My love of folklore has always hummed around in the background. I remember in primary school in Wales we learned about *The Mabinogion*, which is a set of Welsh myths and legends. These stories appear in 14th Century manuscripts but the tales themselves are much older. This colourful cultural heritage has always informed my work.

WALES AND CORNWALL BOTH FEEL LIKE HOME TO ME NOW.

They share wild landscapes and a cultural heritage. As a native Welsh speaker, I instantly noticed similarities between Kernowek and Welsh place names and signs. Both places have a real social history around storytelling. For instance, I'm fascinated by stone circles and the stories that surround them. One of my favourite Cornish legends has to be The Merry Maidens Stone Circle in Penzance. Legend says that a group of maidens were turned to stone as punishment for dancing on a Sunday.

I love storytelling

Hedd yng nghadernid y mynyddoedd mawr

Hedy Y Mynyddoedd by Elin Mannon

ONE OF THE BEST THINGS ABOUT LIVING IN FALMOUTH IS BEING CLOSE TO NATURE.

As an illustrator I draw a lot of inspiration from the land, and I like to borrow colour palettes and textures from the natural world. I might take photographs or bring my little sketchbook with me to document my strolls. I also like to take little pieces of fern or coastal vegetation and sketch from those. It's funny, I even dream about walks now and find myself waking up feeling inspired.

STUDYING AT FALMOUTH MEANS YOU LEARN FROM SOME AMAZING ARTISTS.

I had a tutor in my second year, Rose Forshall, who does some really lovely work for big brands like Anthropologie. It's a great place to do a degree because you're always surrounded by creative people.

I LOVE THE WORK OF ALFRED WALLIS.

It's strange because I tend to be drawn to rich colour palettes and earthy tones, whereas his work is much more muted. But I'm drawn to the naive genre of art and I think his work bridges the gap between traditional art and contemporary illustration.

THERE IS SO MUCH OF THIS COUNTY THAT I'M YET TO DISCOVER.

It's amazing how diverse the Cornish landscape is. Here in Falmouth everything is lush and green, compared to the north coast and The Lizard, which are both wild and atmospheric. I don't have a car, so I rely on public transport or the kindness of friends. Luckily, we're all keen walkers so we regularly head out and explore together.

www.elin-manon.com
@elin_manon_illustration

the INFLUENCER

Rachæl Reid's beautifully curated Instagram feed is a visual tribute to her home county: sunsets over sandy beaches, sleepy villages and misty coves...

WHAT DO YOU DO FOR A LIVING & HOW LONG HAVE YOU LIVED IN CORNWALL?

Hello! I work within my local community to promote education and positive action around waste prevention, re-use and recycling. I've lived in Cornwall for all of my twenty six years.

CAN YOU DESCRIBE YOUR INSTAGRAM IN THREE WORDS?

I had to rope my friends in to help with this one... I think we settled on Romantic, Earthy and Soft. Whatever it is, it has certainly become an accidental love letter to Cornwall.

WHAT'S THE BEST THING ABOUT LIVING IN CORNWALL?

For me, it's the slowness. Living in Cornwall naturally decelerates the pace of modern life. Which isn't for everybody, of course, but I couldn't imagine post-work sea swims not being an option.

ARE THERE ANY DOWNSIDES TO BEING BASED IN A REMOTE PLACE?

Absolutely. Cornwall houses some of the most deprived areas in Europe. Our salaries are low, while house prices remain high. It lacks diversity too: Cornwall is 98.2% white.

WHERE IS THE MOST PHOTOGENIC PLACE IN CORNWALL?

Mousehole & Polperro have my heart. I think tiny fishing villages are absolutely magical; especially out of season in the fog and mizzle. When gift shops are bolted shut, awnings are asleep, and nobody's around — it's so special.

WHAT DO YOU DO TO RELAX?

I wander the coast path, usually in search of a new cove, or a pub. Either is fine!

BEST PLACE TO EAT LOCALLY?

I love a pub with a nice view and outdoor seating. The Pandora Inn in Penzance, and Smugglers Den in Falmouth both immediately spring to mind. I also really enjoy Trevaskis Farm in Hayle for their generous portions and tasty veggies straight from the farm.

WHERE ARE YOUR FAVOURITE PLACES TO SHOP?

Truro's Lemon Street Market for indie shops. Falmouth's Highstreet for homeware (old & new) and antiques. Penzance's Chapel Street for a variety of oddities. Oh, and Hayle in general for a treasure trove of preloved and second-hand shops.

ARE THERE ANY OTHER INSTAGRAM PAGES YOU THINK WE SHOULD CHECK OUT?

Absolutely, there's: @juliaflorenceartist, @curves.and.campervans, @travelandthegirls, @_sarahwoods

Follow Rachael's Cornish adventures on Instagram: @rachaelareid

KERNOW
from above

Matt Warren's unique photographs make you feel like you've been transported to far-flung places: Thailand, Hawaii, Australia, The Seychelles...

Turquoise waters lap against pale white sands and the silhouettes of tiny people pursuing exceptional surf. But don't be fooled, these scenes are closer to home than you'd think. Matt captures Cornwall from a whole new perspective with his aerial photography business: *Kernow From Above.*

01

"Being surrounded by a coast of golden sand and rugged cliff tops it's pretty hard not to be impressed by the views"

– Matt Warren

"Growing up in Cornwall, I was always a beach baby," says Matt Warren. "My parents never had a lot of money, so a day out for us was a day spent on the beach. Honestly, I couldn't thank them enough for it. I loved exploring the rock pools and sand dunes or playing in the sea. I gained a real respect for nature and our oceans. It's hard to explain the feeling I have when I'm out on the coast, but I always feel so at peace. It feels like home."

With 20k Instagram followers and a prestigious British Photography Award under his belt, Matt knows a thing or two about capturing the coastline at its best. From a young age, all he wanted to do was be creative. At first, this manifested as a love for writing music and Matt recalls spending countless hours in a small music studio at his local youth club. He learned to experiment with sounds and get to grips with the latest computer software. But a chance visit from his nephew sent him in a whole new direction...

"I remember my nephew came over one day with this second-hand drone. Straight away I was intrigued by it and I wanted to head out and see what it could do. I'd seen some aerial photography before when I was scrolling through social media, but I assumed it required expensive, specialist equipment. I remember the first time we headed out and I watched the drone take off, fly and capture the most amazing perspectives. From that moment, I knew I had to get my hands on one."

A new chapter of Matt's life began the moment he purchased his own drone and he let his imagination run wild: "It was an excuse to get out and regain my love for nature. The beaches, surf, ports and harbour towns are a dream come true to an aerial photographer. Of course, the moors and woodland can be equally as impressive. I love how Cornwall changes through the different seasons. The calm vibrant seas in the summer can look just as interesting as the moody frantic seas in the winter".

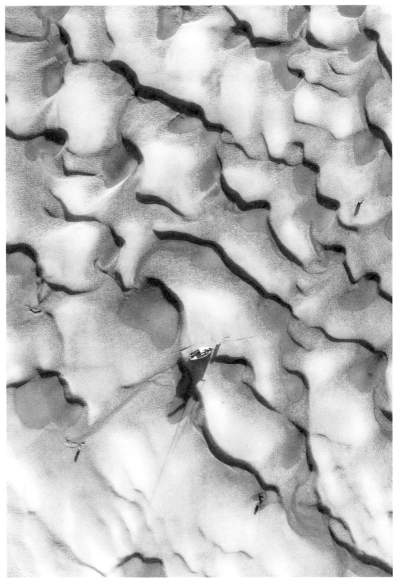

Of course, taking to the skies isn't always plain sailing. In order to use a drone, you need to be au fait with all the associated laws, such as how high and how far you're allowed to fly.

"The basics of flying a drone like mine aren't difficult," says Matt. "But because I wanted to do commercial drone work, I also needed to get a PFCO (permission for commercial operations). This is a week-long course that teaches you about airspace, air navigation and meteorology. You also have to take a theory and flight test, and I had to create an operations manual to show how Kernow From Above would practice."

So far, the response to Matt's unique aerial images has been nothing short of phenomenal. He's built an impressive following on social media and in 2019 his photograph 'Tidal Pools' scooped 'The People's Choice Award' at The British Photography Awards.

"The community here in Cornwall is amazing," he explains. "People love to interact with photographs of the county and without all this community support, Kernow from Above would never have succeeded."

But Matt's success is not entirely down to county pride. His unique images seem to have struck a chord with a much larger audience as well. His choice of vivid colour and his expert eye for capturing hidden gems has attracted an international online audience.

"In the summer months, when the water is super clear and colourful, people sometimes mistake my images for somewhere more tropical," Matt explains. "Of course, I edit my images too. I see it as just as much of an art as I do photography. It also means I can create my own style and try to be even more unique with my imagery!"

Moving forward, we can expect to see plenty more from Kernow from Above. Matt is always experimenting with new ideas and is currently dabbling in the world of aerial video. His client base is varied and any given day you will find him photographing beaches, snapping sporting events or capturing the coast in his own unique way.

If you'd like to purchase Matt's work, you can buy prints from just £35 at kernowfromabove.co.uk.

To keep up-to-date with Matt's work, follow Kernow from Above on Instagram at @kernow_from_above

CIRCLE
Contemporary Gallery

OUR EDITOR PAYS A VISIT TO CIRCLE CONTEMPORARY GALLERY AT **HAWKSFIELD** TO
DISCOVER HOW LAND & SEA INSPIRE A UNIQUE TRIBE OF ARTISTS

Stepping out of the hot August sun and into CIRCLE Gallery is quite the juxtaposition. At Hawksbridge, businesses are housed behind industrial-chic façades, with sun-bleached wooden panels and eye-catching metal signage. But step inside CIRCLE and you're greeted by pared-back interiors, crisp white walls and contemporary artwork.

As I was welcomed by gallerist Lucy Thorman, I took the opportunity to glance around. At once, I was reminded of a stylish London gallery, and yet there was a conspicuous absence of any pretention. To our left, I spied row upon row of neatly spaced white-washed shelves, show-casing affordable artwork by local and international artists. A large-scale woodcut print by Pine Feroda immediately caught my eye thanks

to its eye-pleasing colour palette and its dramatic depiction of ferocious January waves. There was also an eye-popping explosion of colour, courtesy of Spencer Shakespeare's gloriously abstract ode to mother nature (more on this later).

As you walk through the bright and airy space, you can't help but feel like you've left behind the rugged backdrop of North Cornwall and stepped right into a slick Mayfair venue. But despite this shift in perspective, Lucy assured me that the Cornish landscape was not forgotten, and a common conceptual thread tied the entire collection together.

"All the work we showcase here – be it paintings, prints, sculptures or ceramics – take some form of inspira-tion from nature," she explained. "We

01. Simon Gaiger 'Wild Goose' Cedar and lime wash bench with metal legs & Spencer Shakespeare 'Dreaming Of Palm Beach' Oil, gesso on canvas, 200 x 200 cm

have a distinct style that is shaped by artists and artisans who live and work in country and coastal places."

As we climbed the gallery stairs, I started to see a pattern emerging. We stopped at a particularly unique piece of art by local ceramic artist Jenny Beavan. Three tall ceramic poles that bore an uncanny resemblance to silver birch trees stood out from the pristine white wall. It was almost as if someone had plucked the trees from the landscape and placed them there to stop you in your tracks. Alongside this piece, Lucy had hung a particularly captivating woodcut by Pine Feroda entitled 'Sea Change'; an almost hallucinogenic rendering of an enormous crashing wave.

"As you'll see, each artist shares a deep connection with the natural world," Lucy told me. "Whether they are walkers, surfers, divers, botanists, geologists or bird watchers – everything has been created by artists who live surrounded by an expanse of land and sea."

She went on to explain that artists at CIRCLE are represented in two categories: CIRCLE Core and CIRCLE Guest. Talent from both categories come from far and wide, so some of the art on display is created by local Cornish artists, as well as international names from places such as Serbia, Egypt, America and Australia.

As far as CIRCLE's core group of artists is concerned, Lucy explained that their work typically falls into one of three categories: *The Human Landscape, The Landscape of Pleasure,* and *The Material Landcape*. Feeling a little out of my depth, I asked her to expand on these ideas.

"From a city dweller's perspective, landscape-inspired art is often dismissed as 'romantic' and 'unquestioning'," she told me. "But we believe that art born from a true dialogue with nature is life affirming, ever present and continually evolving. We feel that this is best understood through these three conceptual categories."

John O'Carroll perfectly encapsulates *The Human Landscape* through his work. From his cleverly concealed studio on the top floor of the gallery, John creates wide-angle gestural paintings influenced and inspired by the landscapes around him. With studios in Dakleh Oasis (Egypt) and here in Cornwall, John can explore a range of unique landscapes, both cultural and physical, with an emphasis on combining historical and contemporary painting techniques. His work expresses a deep connection and understanding of the spaces through which he has travelled and lived.

02. Jenny Beavan's ceramic Cores alongside 'Sea Change' by Pine Feroda

03. Spencer Shakespeare 'Winter Garden' Acrylic, gesso, pencil on wood panel, 60 x 40 cm

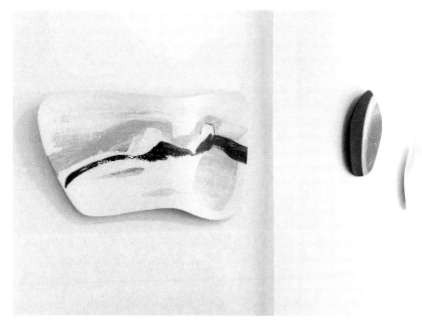

04. John O'carroll 'Place Series' Gesso, Pigment, Copper Leaf On Bent Panels.

The work of CIRCLE artist, Spencer Shakespeare, also depicts *The Human Landscape*. Shakespeare discovered his addiction to the natural world during his yearly holidays to Cornwall which, after 20 years of living on Australia's Gold Coast, he returned to and now resides near Penzance. Spencer's colourful and playful paintings are often a response to places of intersection — the coastline, the edge of forests, sometimes even his own garden — as well as his own imagination. His abstract canvases showcase the blurred boundaries of the world he sees around him: a door, if you like, into a wonderland.

As we continued to look around the space, a flash of vibrant colour against the pale wall introduced me to the work of Susan Bleakley. Her large abstract paintings no doubt represent *The Landscape of Pleasure*. Susan's work is nuanced and beautiful, utilising a technique known as 'simultaneous contrast' to great effect. Her choice of colour reflects the Atlantic light she sees from her studio window and is synergetic with the flowers and foliage that grow in her Cornish clifftop garden.

Throughout the gallery, it's easy to spot art that represents *The Material Landscape*: artists who quite literally use the natural environment for inspiration and making. For example, sculptor Simon Gaiger creates free forms and furniture from fallen trees and abandoned metal; keeping the evidence of past use in his work.

There's also the unmistakable Pine Feroda. Not to be mistaken for a single artist, Pine Feroda is the collective name used by three British artists (Merlyn Chesterman, Ian Phillips and Judith Westcott), who together create large-scale, dramatic woodcut prints inspired by the extraordinary coastlines of North Devon and Cornwall. Craggy rock formations, tumultuous waves and the interplay of light and water are all explored through their unique work. The trio can often be seen on their local beaches and headlands, collectively drawing on clifftops, or in the ocean itself. Of all the work that has been carefully curated by Lucy and John O'Carroll at CIRCLE, these striking Pine Feroda prints are among my favourite.

As we came to the end of my gallery tour, Lucy showed me the latest addition to CIRCLE: a beautifully curated collection of ceramics, including a number of pieces by renowned Cornish ceramicist, Chris Prindl. Lucy is excited that the artefacts will add more diversity to the gallery, showcasing traditional craftmanship alongside contempo-

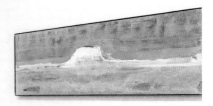

05. John O'Carroll 'Place Series' Gesso, pigment, copper leaf on panel (Exhibition View)

the gallery, showcasing traditional craftmanship alongside contemporary art. All ceramics will available to purchase through the gallery website, in order to make them more accessible to a wider audience. With big brands like Anthropolgie and Soho Home catching on to the beauty of stoneware, it seems only fair that independent makers ought to be celebrated too.

As we descended the gallery steps once again, Lucy explained why she feels that CIRCLE is one-of-a-kind: "The response to this tribe of artists has been hugely positive thus far. We have a loyal following of interior designers and art collectors who work with us time and again. It's extremely important to build those genuine connections with our clients."

Truthfully, CIRCLE Contemporary Gallery isn't comparable to the tourist-trap venues of St Ives and the south coast.

Cornish art seems to have become synonymous with postcard-perfect scenes and cheery nautical prints. Artwork that is bought alongside clotted cream fudge and sea glass trinkets isn't necessarily showcasing the outstanding class of artists that the county has nurtured over time.

CIRCLE's small collective of local artists and international creators are committed to celebrating art that is made in harmony with nature. In an age when environmental sustainability and climate change are among the most pressing topics of our time, CIRCLE sets a strong example and elevates conscious creators. This is a gallery that would not be out of place on a busy metropolitan street in London; wyet it perfectly encapsulates the contemporary Cornish art scene, with its roots very firmly planted in the land.

Visit CIRCLE at Hawksfield Wadebridge PL27 7LR or circlecontemporary.co.uk

06. CIRCLE Contemporary Gallery Interior (closest artwork by Peter Hayes)

To enquire about any of the artwork featured email lucy@circlecontemporary.co.uk

WILD
food

Rachæl Brown steps off the beaten track as she goes foraging in Fowey with Cornish Wild Food.

The fact it's one of the hottest days in August doesn't bother us as we cool in the shade of a National Trust car park near Fowey. Our group of seven listen and nod in the dappled woodland, skin sun-creamed and backs rucksacked, bonded together with by shared curiosity of the outdoors.

Matt, our cheerful guide and guru of all sprouting things — complete with lockdown beard — runs through some guidelines before he leads us down through the woodland to the sea. What we will find in between these two destinations is still uncertain. Unhelpfully, all I can muster to imagine is us chewing on salty fronds of seaweed.

Although we embark along a narrow country road under arching tree branches, Matt emphasises that wild food can be found on your walk into town. Not long after leaving the car park we find some. We pluck a green leaf from the hedgerow and Matt instructs us to wait for each other before taking a bite.

At first, biting into the leaf takes a small amount of mental effort, pushing past my rational barriers of what's edible. Then a zing shocks my palate. It has a very intense but pleasant sourness, like granny smith apples. The leaf is wood sorrel. It's a name I've only seen in old books and didn't realise it grew around me.

Passing through a gate into darker woodland, we begin our descent down a slim trail to the coast. As Matt reaches for a natural fungi firelighter hanging from a tree branch he relays not just its

different names but the largely forgotten stories, histories and properties that have fallen out of common knowledge. As we walk we learn more. Particular leaves start to stand out in the bushes and woodland, adding personality to what used to be a monotonous green blur.

The path flattens out into grassland and the first glimpses of distant boats drift into view. Ornamental white umbels (umbrella shaped) of wild carrot grow here, and crushing their tiny fragrant flower buds under the nail releases a citrusy spice, which, according to Matt, is ideal for aromatic curries. Flavouring a curry with spices from English grasslands seems a strange idea, but I welcome it.

As we finally hoist ourselves onto the shingle beach, our bags lumpy with different stalks and leaves, we find more

wild food. Clumps of rock samphire protrude out of the cliff's sharp lines.

They taste intensely of the beach with a lemony aftertaste. Mouth ringing with strong new flavours, I feel borderline irritation at the variety of free food and wild spices I've spent years absentmindedly walking past.

Matt stresses that responsible foraging is a skill we can all learn and I think of the plants that perhaps I couldn't live off of, but I could use to make jams, spiced flapjacks, dandelion wine, caffeine drinks, fresh salads, tempura vegetables and aromatic curries. Far more exciting than limp seaweed!

Want to book your own foraging walk with Cornish Wild Food? Go to: www.cornishwildfood.co.uk

Wild Swimming

Rachæl Brown discovers some of the most thrilling wild swimming spots in Cornwall.

Although some wild swimming purists might disagree with the saltwater swims included on this list, we're sure any disagreements will melt away when they see the ocean.

Sea pools or giant rockpools are good places to start for beginners, before you build up to a skinny dip in a river...

Porthtowan Seapool

If the tide is far out enough, it's easier to approach this seapool from sandy Porthtowan beach by clambering up a cluster of rocks. It's a smaller secluded pool, hidden around the side of the bay, but finding it is rewarding. Deep enough to dive in, it's a nice spot for gazing at anemones.

Grebe (Helford River)

You can reach this unspoilt stretch of shoreline by parking in Bosveal and following the woodland walk towards the river. You'll reach a pebbly band of beach with clear, peaceful water, framed with lush woodlands and a couple of rockpools. Usually still and a bit warmer than the sea, the coves and inlets of the Helford river are reliable spots for wild swimming. Feel free to follow the coast round to Durgan for a pit stop.

Kynance Cove

Two miles north of Lizard Point lies Kynance Cove. Its aquamarine waters make it a popular tourist destination which means there is limited parking. Arrive early or walk down on the south west coast path to guarantee being able to stop. Plan your arrival for when the tide is going out to properly explore the caves, azure waters and Asparagus island.

Lansallos Cove

This sandy shingle crescent is enclosed by folding cliffs and clear blue sea. To get to the cove, set off on the wooded trail from Lansallos, it's signposted by the church and Victory Cottage. The coast around Lantic and Lantivet Bay has a wealth of coves for swimming in, so explore and find your own secret spots along the coast path. Look out for Reed Water waterfall, also in Lansallos cove.

Treyarnon Bay Rockpool

This large natural rockpool is deep enough to plunge into and wide enough to swim lengths, a great introduction for beginners who want to immerse themselves in nature whilst avoiding any strong waves or currents. Scramble over the rocky areas on the side of the beach to find it.

Bodmin Parkway, River Fowey

Behind the train station, one of the bends in the River Fowey swells, running deep enough for a refreshing freshwater dip. Walk along the leafy riverside to this secret spot and look out for a deeper space to submerge. As with all swims, judge the level and flow of the water before getting in.

RELAXATION

essentials

01. Reusable Bamboo Face Wipes

Cornish artisan Helen Round has designed these beautiful eco-friendly, reusable face wipes. They're perfect for your daily cleansing ritual and great for popping in your travel bag.

www.helenround.com

02. Land & Water Bath & Body Oil

This sustainably made bath and body oil by Land & Water contains warming orange and ginger, along with mood-boosting black pepper and geranium essential oils. Add a capful to your bath to soothe away the aches of a day well spent.

land-and-water.co.uk

03. St Eval Thyme & Mint Candle

These St Eval candles are hand-poured with the rejuvenating scent of crushed garden mint and herbal thyme. Once used, the terracotta pots can be filled with soil to create your very own window sill herb garden.

www.st-eval.com

04. Serenity Pulse Point Roll On

This mini Bloom Remedies pulse point roll on contains a soothing blend of ylang ylang, geranium, sweet orange, cedarwood, lavender and patchouli. These serene scents are known to soothe the nervous system and aid relaxation and sleep.

www.bloomremedies.co.uk

05. Lychee & Rose Handwash

We love the lifeology range at Marks & Spencer. A luxurious addition to any bathroom, this beautifully scented handwash is formulated to soothe your skin and uplift your senses.

www.marksandspencer.com

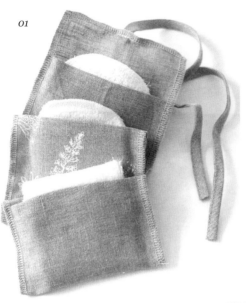

01

02

land & water.

BATH & BODY OIL

Orange, Ginger & Geranium
with sea buckthorn oil

03

LIFEOLOGY

LYCHEE & ROSE
FRAGRANCE BURST
HAND WASH

05

BLOOM
remedies

Serenity
Pulse Point Roll On

Organic
W...ng
...rnwall

BLOOM
remedies

Serenity
Pulse Point Roll On

04

Great Cornish Food

The Cornish Chef puts the county's finest ingredients to the test in this veritable feast using produce from The Great Cornish Food Store.

PHOTOGRAPHY & STYLING: ALI GREEN

Cornish Pizza Two Ways

Few dishes are easier to make and as instantly satisfying as homemade pizza. Here, The Cornish Chef shares his fool proof dough recipe, alongside two delicious topping ideas to please meat lovers and vegetarians alike.

PIZZA DOUGH

125g strong white flour

75ml tepid water

½ tsp dried fast-action yeast

½ tsp salt

½ tbsp olive oil

PESTO & HEN EGG PIZZA

190ml jar of green pesto

400g spinach, cooked & chilled

1 courgette, sliced & roasted

100g extra mature Gouda

1 St. Ewe Rich Egg

Making The Pizza Dough

1. Mix the flour in a bowl with the tepid water, salt, yeast and oil. Mix into a ball and then knead on a floured surface - stretching the dough out and bringing back into a ball - for around 10 mins until the dough feels springy.

2. When fully kneaded, place the dough into a bowl, cover with cling film and leave somewhere warm until the dough doubles in size – approximately 30 mins.

3. Preheat your oven to 240C / gas 9 and heat a baking tray or pizza stone, then roll the dough into a rough disk with a little lip around the edge. Place your base on a chopping board or pizza peel, ready for your choice of toppings.

To Make The Pesto & Hen Egg Pizza

1. Combine the green pesto and cooked spinach in a bowl, before spreading over the pizza dough base. Scatter with the cooked courgette slices and grate over the Gouda.

2. Slide into the hot oven and bake for 5 mins before removing and cracking an egg onto the middle. Return the pizza to the oven for 4-6 mins, until golden and cooked with a runny yolk.

TOMATO SAUCE

150g tomato paste

400g tomato sauce

2 tbsp oregano

2 tbsp Italian seasoning

½ tsp garlic powder

1 pinch of sea salt

Cracked black pepper

1 tsp caster sugar

CHARCUTERIE PIZZA

100g mixed charcuterie

75g Cornish brie

25g extra mature Gouda

100g rocket

30g pine nuts

1 lemon

To Make The Charcuterie Pizza

1. Make your tomato sauce by mixing all the ingredients in a bowl. Spread a thin layer of the sauce over the base and top with the charcuterie, followed by the brie and Gouda.

2. Slide into the preheated oven and bake for between 8-12 mins, until golden. While the pizza is cooking, toss the rocket and pine nuts in a bowl with the zest and juice of a lemon. When the pizza is cooked, serve with the zesty rocket on top.

Recommendations: The Cornish Chef uses a mix of Cornish Charcuterie and Deli Farm Charcuterie for added variety.

Chilli & Ginger Crab Cakes

A kick of chilli and fragrant ginger take delicate crab meat to the next level in this dish. If possible, begin the crab cakes the day before or as many hours as you can spare.

SERVES 4

THE CRAB CAKES

350g mashed potatoes, cooled

500g cooked Cornish crab meat

A thumb-sized piece of ginger

2 spring onions, thinly sliced

1 red chilli, finely chopped

Pinch of Cornish Sea Salt

Pinch of white pepper

1 large St Ewe egg

Hard Pressed Rapeseed Oil

Plain flour, for dusting

THE AIOLI

1 tbsp white wine vinegar

2 egg yolks

1 lime

200ml rapeseed oil

TO SERVE

2 limes

Bad Boy Chilli Jam

1. Make the crab cakes by combining the mash and crab meat in a large bowl. Finely grate the ginger and add to the mix along with the spring onions and chopped chilli. Season to taste with sea salt and white pepper. Crack in the egg and mix well to integrate and bind together.

2. Shape the crab cakes into four patties before placing them onto a lined baking tray. Leave in the fridge overnight, if possible, or for at least 1 hour to firm up.

3. Make the aioli using a food processor. In the bowl, combine the vinegar, egg yolk and the zest and juice of one lime. Turn the machine on and slowly pour in the oil. Once all the oil has been added, taste the mixture and adjust the seasoning if necessary. Place the aioli in a sealed container and keep in the fridge until needed.

4. Preheat the oven to 180C / gas 4. Dust the crab cakes with flour and a pinch of salt, before heating a glug of rapeseed oil in a frying pan over a high heat. When the oil is hot, fry the crab cakes in batches without overcrowding the pan. When golden on both sides, transfer to the oven and leave for around 10 mins to cook through the middle.

5. In the meantime, prepare four plates with a salad of your choice. We like to use watercress and radish, with lime wedges, a dollop of aioli and a spoonful of chilli jam. Enjoy the crab cakes hot from the oven!

Creamy Cornish Panna Cotta
with Saffron & Honey Poached Pears

This decadent panna cotta is hands down one of the tastiest desserts we've ever tried. The recipe uses Roddas Creamery clotted cream, Cornish Saffron, Tregothnan honey and Furniss fairings.

SERVES 4

THE PANNA COTTA

2 leaves of gelatine
300ml double cream
50ml milk
175g clotted cream
70g caster sugar
1 vanilla pod
100g Cornish Fairings

FOR THE PEARS

4 pears
1 litre of water
250g caster sugar
50g honey
1 stick of cinnamon
2 star anise
1 tsp vanilla paste
Pinch of Cornish Saffron

1. Begin by making the panna cottas, at least 8 hours ahead of serving. Place the gelatine leaves in a small bowl of cold water and set aside. In a medium, heavy-bottomed saucepan, heat the double cream, milk, clotted cream and sugar, along with the vanilla pod (scrape out the seeds and add to the mix).

2. Heat the mixture until nearly simmering and then remove from the heat and allow to cool for 10 mins. Squeeze the water out of the gelatine leaves and add to the cream mix before whisking thoroughly until dissolved. Pour the mix into a jug and transfer into your choice of either a dessert mould or a glass. Place in the fridge until needed.

3. Peel the pears - leaving the stalks on - and combine in a medium saucepan with all the other ingredients. Simmer on a medium-low heat until the pears are tender - check with the tip of a knife, it should take roughly 45 mins. When the pears are done, remove from the pan with a slotted spoon and set aside to cool.

4. Increase the heat under the remaining liquid to medium and continuing to simmer until it has reduced by three quarters. Take off the heat and remove the cinnamon stick and star anise before setting aside to cool. Place the pears in the fridge until needed but keep the syrup at room temperature.

5. When you're ready to serve, remove the panna cottas from the fridge and free them from their moulds. Present the pears alongside the panna cottas and pour over a little of the syrup. Scatter the crumbled fairings over the top to complete the dessert.

Great Cornish Food Store

Truro

If the Cornish Chef's recipes got your taste buds tingling, we suggest paying a visit to The Great Food Store to stock up on fresh and local ingredients. Located alongside Waitrose in Truro, this beautiful, independent grocery store contains its own butchery, fishmonger and chef led cafe, deli and takeaway.

The store is passionate about supporting the local economy and putting the joy back into grocery shopping. So, you can expect a personal service and a carefully selected range of produce. On the shelves you'll find a myriad of exceptional food and drink suppliers from all over Cornwall, including artisan cheeses, Cornish saffron, charcuterie and local spirits.

Buying from the deli counter is a lot like having your own personal chef. There's a colourful range of salads, main meals, side dishes and puds on offer, each crafted with the very best local ingredients. Better still, you can also grab a sandwich or hand-made pastry to go, or enjoy a barista-brewed Origin Coffee from the fabulous onsite café.

Tregurra Park, Newquay Road
Truro, TR1 1RH

greatcornishfood.co.uk

Blood Orange Cosmo

As well as fantastic food producers, Cornwall is home to some iconic drinks brands. Tarquin's Gin has become one of the region's most recognizable exports, and this easy-to-recreate cocktail uses their delicious 'Cornish Sunshine' Blood Orange Gin.

50ml Tarquin's Blood Orange Gin

35ml cranberry juice

10ml lemon juice

1 egg white or 25ml aquafaba

Ice

EQUIPMENT

A cocktail shaker

Strainer

A coupe cocktail glass

1. Add the gin, cranberry juice and lemon juice to a cocktail shaker with a good scoop of ice. Put the top on the shaker.

2. Give it a good shake until it feels cold in your hand, around 10-15 seconds.

3. Strain to remove the ice and return the cocktail to the shaker.

4. Add the egg white and give it a good shake without any ice. This is called a dry shake and will foam up the egg white.

5. Pour the contents of the shaker into the coupe class to serve.

Legends of Cornwall

Cornwall's wild and rugged landscape has breathed life into a wealth of myths and legends. In this land of magic and intrigue, you need only scratch the surface to uncover a unique folkloric past.

ILLUSTRATIONS: ELIN MANNON

The Cornish certainly have a knack for storytelling. Perhaps it's in their blood or perhaps there's something in the water. But after a pint of Rattler has loosened their tongue, most Cornish folk have a story to tell about their local town. Every harbour has a ghostly galleon, materialising in the night only to melt away in the mists of dawn. Mermaids and piskies colour familiar tales and such stories are so pervasive it's hard to unpick the annals of history from local legend...

GIANTS

Cornwall is the fabled home of giants, monstrous men who were miles tall and prone to fits of rage. These enormous creatures are often used to explain the unexplainable, such as unique geographic landmarks or unusual stone remains. Tales reference giants carving colossal seats out of the earth or hurling humongous boulders at one another. These brutes inhabited the land long before man and the first legendary ruler of Cornwall, Corineus, supposedly had to fight the giant Gogmagog to solidify his rule.

St Michael's Mount is said to have once been home to the giant Cormoran and his long-suffering wife, Cormelian. Their tale states that, centuries ago, Mount's Bay was covered by a thick, foreboding forest and Cormoran insisted that his wife help him quarry granite to build a mound in the middle on which to live.

One day, Cormoran decided to take a nap and left his wife to shoulder the burden of work. Tired of following his backbreaking orders, Cormelian shook the heavy granite boulders from her apron pockets and replaced them with lighter, green stones. When her cruel husband woke, he realised what she had done and punished her with a rough shove. The green stones you'll see at St Michael's Mount today are said to have fallen there when Cormelian's apron strings broke and scattered the rocks to the forest floor.

But the spiteful Cormoran got his just deserts when the bay flooded, leaving him to live alone on the granite island they had created. He would regularly wade ashore to steal livestock from nearby farmers or disturb the local community by fighting and bickering with other giants.

The locals grew tired of Cormoran's antics, and a reward was offered to anyone who could kill the boulder-throwing brute. A farmer's boy named Jack rose to the challenge, creeping onto the Mount one night and digging a huge deep pit. He disguised the trap with sticks and leaves and at sunrise he blew his horn to wake the sleeping giant.

Startled by the sudden noise, Cormoran ran out onto the Mount to find the source of the commotion. Failing to see Jack's clever trap, he fell into the pit and found himself buried up to his neck. Jack seized his opportunity to dispose of the giant once and for all and reached for his axe. Legend says he lopped off the giant's head, forever earning the reputation of Jack The Giant-Killer – sound familiar?

THE POBEL VEAN

Along with its giants of mythical proportions, Cornish folklore is filled with references to the Pobel Vean (little people). Chief among these magical, miniature creatures are the Cornish piskies. These tiny, sprite-like creatures are said to roam the countryside of Cornwall and Devon, dancing and making merriment, as well as getting up to all manner of mischief.

Legend states that piskies live in secret, isolated places, such as burrows and stone circles, and are so small they can sit in the palm of your hand or rest in the shade of a toadstool. But what these little characters lack in size, they make up for in their cheeky dispositions.

Piskies are rumoured to lure unsuspecting travellers off moorland or forest paths. They're fiercely protectiveof their homes, and they have been known to get into territorial scuffles with local monks. But piskies are also fickle by nature and can easily be won over with a colourful ribbon or a small token gift. Once suitably pacified, they are said to be helpful creatures who love to dance and sing.

Along with piskies, the Cornish bucca regularly crop up in local lore. These small creatures are said to have inhabited the mines and cliffs of coastal communities. In his extensive research into the faerie folk of Cornwall, 19th century folklorist, William Bottrell, distinguished between two types of bucca - *bucca widn* (white bucca) and *bucca dhu* (black bucca).

Regardless of their nature, it is known that the people of Cornwall were deeply superstitious about these wiry little fellows. In the fishing ports of Newlyn and Mousehole, it was tradition for fishermen to leave out a portion of their catch for the bucca, and in Penzance sailors claimed to hear bucca cries from high up on the cliffs.

A particularly well-known bucca was The Sea Bucca of Lamorna Cove. With skin the colour of a conger eel and a tangled mess of seaweed hair, legend claims he was often spied swimming in the waves or perching on the rocks with the gulls. The lonesome creature was fabled to have once been a handsome human, who was cursed by a jealous witch to live a life of solitude.

As testament of their unpredictable nature, this particular bucca was very fond of children and was known to assist Lamorna fishing boats by driving fish into their nets and crabs into their pots. Yet he was also capable of a terrible rage if you crossed him, so locals made a habit of avoiding him, leaving out the occasional fish or morsel to placate him instead...

MERMAIDS

Beautiful, mysterious and often dangerous, mermaids have an important part to play in Cornish folklore. These alluring sea dwellers are rumoured to have resided in hidden coves, enticing sailors to their untimely demise and somtimes taking human lovers. Sightings of mermaids have been reported as far north as Padstow - where the deadly Doom Bar was apparently formed by a vengeful mermaid - to southernly Seaton. But the most famous Cornish mermaid of all has to be Morveren: The Mermaid of Zennor.

The tiny village of Zennor sits betwixt the moors and the wild North coast, just five miles west of St Ives. Here you'll find the church of St. Senara, home to an intriguing artefact known as the Mermaid's Chair. This wooden bench is believed to be around 600 years old and features an ornate carving of a mermaid with flowing hair. She clutches a comb in one hand and a mirror in the other, making her an unusual sight for an ancient church. The carving is said to commemorate a local tale that goes something like this:

The choristers of St. Senara have always been famed for their beautiful singing, but no one was ever quite as exceptional as the handsome young Mathey Trewhella. Mathey would often lead the congregation in song and his voice was said to be so angelic that folk would come from far and wide to hear him sing.

On one particularly sunny Sunday, his performance drew Morveren from the sea. The mysteious mermaid disguised herself as beautiful human woman and slipped into the back of the church to join the congregation.

During the service, Morveren's own celestial voice caught Mathey's attention. Captivated by his otherworldly admirer, the young singer vowed to learn more about her and at the end of the service, he pursued her back down the coastal path to Pendour Cove. Legend says that Mathey was never seen again, but locals believe that she took him by the hand and the lovestruck pair vanished beneath the waves.

Years later, a ship cast its anchor off the coast of Zennor and the captain heard a woman calling out from the water. To his surprise, she was a mermaid and she asked him to kindly move his ship's anchor. She said that the anchor was resting on the entrance to her home and she could not get inside to see her husband.

The captain obliged and the mermaid vanished once again with a flash of her shimmering tail. When the captain came ashore and told his tale to the patrons of a Zennor tavern, the locals were convinced that the mermaid was the mysterious woman who had led young Mathey Trewhella away many years before...

For more recommendations and ideas for
things to do in Cornwall, visit our website:

www.maverickguide.co.uk